A COOKBOOK TO LOWER HIGH BLOOD PRESSURE FOR BEGINNERS.

AN EASY GUIDE AND DELICIOUS RECIPES TO KEEP YOUR HEART HEALTHY AND HAVE A HEALTHY LIFE.

Dr **Robert C. George**

gained. Therefore, the contents within can neither be stored electronically, transferred, nor kept in a database. Neither in Part nor full can the document be copied, scanned, faxed, or retained without approval from the publisher or creator.

TABLE OF CONTENTS

INTRODUCTION

This cookbook highlights the vital significance of a nutritious diet in treating high blood pressure. It shows the influence of certain nutrients on blood pressure, such as sodium, potassium, magnesium, and fiber. The cookbook illustrates how some food patterns, such as the DASH (Diet Approaches to Stop Hypertension) diet, have been shown successful in decreasing blood pressure.

Here, the cookbook gives realistic suggestions for adopting a blood pressure-friendly diet. It highlights the fundamental concepts, including minimizing salt consumption, boosting potassium-rich meals, including whole grains, prioritizing fruits and vegetables, selecting lean meats, and limiting saturated fats and cholesterol. The part also highlights the significance of portion management and mindful eating.

To encourage readers in implementing a blood pressure-friendly diet, this cookbook includes practical recommendations for grocery shopping and meal planning. It helps read food labels to detect high-sodium goods, proposes healthier choices, and advocates integrating a range of fresh, seasonal fruit. It also discusses how to plan meals, establish shopping lists, and guarantee a well-balanced diet.

The cookbook dives into culinary practices that help reduced blood pressure. It covers techniques such as steaming, grilling, baking, and stir-frying that help preserve nutrients while lowering the need for excessive fats or salt. The section gives useful advice on flavoring foods using herbs, spices, and natural ingredients to increase taste without sacrificing healthfulness.

Recognizing varied tastes and nutritional limitations, this book invites readers to customize the recipes to fit their choices and needs. It advises substitutes and adaptations, such as gluten-free choices, vegetarian or vegan variants, and tips for decreasing added sugars. The cookbook invites experimentation and customization while maintaining faithful to the fundamentals of a blood pressure-friendly diet.

By giving a complete knowledge of high blood pressure and its link with nutrition, along with practical ideas and advice, this introductory chapter sets the tone for the remainder of the cookbook. It allows readers to make educated decisions and prepares them for the tasty and health-promoting dishes that follow in the following chapters.

CHAPTER 1
BREAKFAST RECIPES

Spinach and Mushroom Egg White Omelet

Start your day with a healthful and tasty spinach and mushroom egg white omelet. This dish blends the benefits of leafy greens and mushrooms with the lightness of egg whites, offering a protein-packed and low-fat breakfast choice that promotes healthy blood pressure.

Ingredients:

4 big egg whites

1 cup fresh spinach, finely chopped ½ cup sliced mushrooms

1 small onion, chopped

1 garlic clove, minced

1 teaspoon olive oil

Salt and pepper according to preference

Instructions:

Heat a non-stick skillet over medium heat and add the olive oil.

Add the chopped onion and minced garlic to the skillet. Sauté for 2-3 minutes until the onion turns transparent and aromatic.

Add the sliced mushrooms to the pan and simmer for another 2-3 minutes until they soften and lose their moisture.

Stir in the chopped spinach and heat for a further minute until wilted. Season with salt and pepper to taste. Remove the veggies from the skillet and put aside.

In a mixing dish, beat the egg whites until they become foamy and form soft peaks.

Heat the same skillet over medium heat and gently coat it with cooking spray.

Pour the whisked egg whites into the skillet, ensuring they distribute evenly.

Cook the egg whites for approximately 2 minutes until they start to firm around the edges.

Gently spoon the sautéed veggies onto one side of the omelet.

Carefully fold the other side of the omelet over the veggies, forming a half-moon shape. Press down lightly with a spatula.

Cook for an extra minute to ensure the omelet is cooked through and set.

Slide the omelet onto a platter and let it cool for a minute before serving.

Garnish with extra salt and pepper if desired.

Enjoy your delicious and heart-healthy spinach and mushroom egg white omelet!

This omelet is full of vitamins, minerals, and antioxidants from spinach and mushrooms while being low in cholesterol and saturated fat thanks to the usage of egg whites. It's a delightful and nutritious way to start your day and assist your efforts in keeping good blood pressure levels.

Whole Wheat Banana Pancakes

Indulge in a wonderful and healthful morning with these whole-wheat banana pancakes. They are a nutritional alternative to typical pancakes, delivering complex carbs, dietary fiber, and natural sweetness from ripe bananas. These pancakes are a terrific way to integrate whole grains into your diet while keeping your blood pressure in line.

Ingredients:

1 cup whole wheat flour

1 teaspoon baking powder

½ teaspoon baking soda

¼ teaspoon salt

1 ripe banana, mashed

1 cup low-fat milk (or dairy-free substitute)

1 big egg

1 tablespoon honey or maple syrup (optional)

Cooking spray or a tiny bit of oil for greasing

Instructions:

In a large mixing basin, combine the whole wheat flour, baking powder, baking soda, and salt. Mix thoroughly to ensure the dry ingredients are uniformly distributed.

In a separate dish, mash the ripe banana until smooth.

Add the mashed banana, low-fat milk, egg, and honey (or maple syrup) to the dry ingredient combination. Stir until all the ingredients are fully blended, but be cautious not to overmix. The batter should be somewhat lumpy.

Let the batter sit for 5 minutes to let the whole wheat flour absorb the liquid.

Meanwhile, prepare a non-stick skillet or griddle over medium heat.

Lightly coat the pan or griddle with cooking spray or a little quantity of oil.

Pour approximately ¼ cup of batter into the griddle for each pancake.

Cook until bubbles form on the surface of the pancake and the edges start to appear firm, which normally takes 2-3 minutes.

Flip the pancakes gently with a spatula and cook for a further 1-2 minutes on the other side until golden brown.

Transfer the fried pancakes to a platter and keep them warm while you prepare the remaining batter.

Serve the whole wheat banana pancakes with your choice of toppings such as fresh berries, sliced bananas, a drizzle of honey or maple syrup, or a dollop of Greek yogurt.

These whole wheat banana pancakes are not only tasty but also give the advantages of whole grains and the natural sweetness of bananas. They provide a pleasant and healthful breakfast alternative that is lower in refined carbs and higher in fiber compared to regular pancakes. Enjoy them guilt-free as part of your blood pressure-friendly diet.

Chia Seed Pudding with Berries

Indulge in a creamy and healthy chia seed pudding with a blast of fresh berries. This dish combines the nutritional advantages of chia seeds, such as omega-3 fatty acids and fiber, with the antioxidant-rich richness of berries. It's a tasty and fulfilling breakfast alternative that helps your blood pressure objectives.

Ingredients:

¼ cup chia seeds

1 cup unsweetened almond milk (or your chosen milk)

1 tablespoon honey or maple syrup

½ teaspoon vanilla extract

Assorted fresh berries (e.g., strawberries, blueberries, raspberries)

Instructions:

In a dish or container, blend the chia seeds, almond milk, honey (or maple syrup), and vanilla essence.

Whisk the mixture carefully to ensure the chia seeds are uniformly dispersed.

Let the mixture settle for approximately 5 minutes, then whisk again to break up any clumps.

Cover the dish or jar and refrigerate for at least 2 hours, or ideally overnight, to enable the chia seeds to absorb the liquid and develop a pudding-like consistency. Stir or shake the mixture several times during this period to avoid clumping.

Once the chia seed pudding has thickened to your preferred consistency, give it a vigorous stir.

Serve the chia seed pudding in separate dishes or jars.

Top each dish with a liberal handful of fresh berries, such as sliced strawberries, blueberries, or raspberries.

For more texture and taste, you may sprinkle some additional chia seeds, shredded coconut, or chopped almonds on top.

Enjoy the chia seed pudding with berries as a delightful and nutrient-packed breakfast or snack.

This chia seed pudding with berries is a terrific way to include the nutritional benefits of chia seeds and antioxidant-rich berries into your diet. It gives a creamy and pleasant texture while being low in saturated fat and cholesterol. Enjoy this tasty and heart-healthy delicacy as part of your blood pressure-friendly eating plan.

Each breakfast meal in this chapter attempts to give a healthy and balanced start to the day, integrating whole grains, fruits, and vegetables while avoiding extra salt, saturated fats, and cholesterol. The cookbook invites readers to experiment with tastes and toppings to suit their preferences while sticking to the principles of a blood pressure-friendly diet. With these recipes, readers may begin their mornings with wholesome and tasty breakfasts that help their general well-being.

CHAPTER 2
APPETIZERS AND SNACKS

Cucumber and Yogurt Dip with Whole Wheat Pita Bread

This section features a delicious and healthful appetizer dish including a cucumber and yogurt dip served with whole wheat pita bread. This light and tasty snack alternative is low in salt and saturated fats while giving a delightful crunch and creamy texture.

Ingredients:

1 big cucumber, peeled, seeded, and coarsely diced

1 cup plain Greek yogurt

2 cloves of garlic, minced

1 tablespoon fresh lemon juice

1 tablespoon fresh dill, chopped

Salt and pepper to taste

Whole wheat pita bread, sliced into triangles, for serving

Instructions:

In a medium-sized bowl, mix the diced cucumber, Greek yogurt, minced garlic, fresh lemon juice, and chopped dill.

Mix vigorously until all the ingredients are thoroughly blended.

Season with salt and pepper to taste.

Cover the bowl and chill the cucumber and yogurt dip for at least 30 minutes to enable the flavors to melt together.

Once cooled, give the dip a last swirl before serving.

Arrange the whole wheat pita bread triangles on a serving tray.

Serve the cucumber and yogurt dip beside the pita bread.

Dip the pita bread into the cool cucumber and yogurt combination and enjoy!

This cucumber and yogurt dip is a lovely way to integrate veggies and probiotic-rich yogurt into your diet. The use of whole wheat pita bread provides fiber and minerals, making it a healthier option than normal refined flour bread. This appetizer is ideal for entertaining or as a light snack choice that supports your efforts to maintain good blood pressure levels.

Roasted Red Pepper Hummus with Vegetable Sticks

The cookbook provides a recipe for roasted red pepper hummus combined with a colorful selection of veggie sticks. This appetizer is rich in fiber, vitamins, and minerals, making it a healthful alternative for dipping and nibbling.

Ingredients:

1 can (15 ounces) chickpeas, drained and rinsed

1 roasted red pepper, peeled and seeded

2 tablespoons tahini

2 teaspoons fresh lemon juice

2 cloves of garlic, minced

1 tablespoon olive oil

½ teaspoon ground cumin

Salt and pepper to taste

Assorted vegetable sticks (carrots, celery, bell peppers, cucumber) for serving

Instructions:

In a food processor, mix the drained and rinsed chickpeas, roasted red pepper, tahini, fresh lemon juice, chopped garlic, olive oil, ground cumin, salt, and pepper.

Process the mixture until smooth and creamy, scraping down the edges as required.

Taste the hummus and adjust the spice if required.

Transfer the hummus to a serving dish.

Prepare the vegetable sticks by cutting carrots, celery, bell peppers, and cucumber into thin, easy-to-dip sticks.

Arrange the veggie sticks around the hummus dish.

Serve the roasted red pepper hummus with veggie sticks for a colorful and healthful snack option.

This roasted red pepper hummus gives a delightful way to integrate legumes, like chickpeas, into your diet, which is a terrific source of protein and fiber. Coupled with the choice of veggie sticks, this appetizer provides a pleasant and healthful alternative to commercial munchies. It's an excellent alternative for people trying to regulate their blood pressure while enjoying a tasty and nutrient-rich snack.

Baked Sweet Potato Chips

These chips are a nutritional alternative to regular fried potato chips, delivering fiber, vitamins, and minerals while being low in salt and harmful fats.

Ingredients:

2 medium sweet potatoes, cleaned and peeled

1 tablespoon olive oil

½ teaspoon paprika

½ teaspoon garlic powder

½ teaspoon salt

Freshly ground black pepper to taste

Instructions:

Preheat the oven to 400°F (200°C) and line two baking sheets with parchment paper.

Using a mandolin slicer or a sharp knife, slice the sweet potatoes into thin, even rounds.

In a large bowl, combine the sweet potato slices with olive oil, paprika, garlic powder, salt, and black pepper. Make sure each slice is covered with the oil and spices.

Arrange the sweet potato slices in a single layer on the prepared baking pans, ensuring they don't overlap.

Bake the sweet potato chips in the preheated oven for 15-20 minutes, or until they are crisp and faintly brown, rotating them midway through the baking time.

Keep a watchful check on the chips as they may rapidly go from crispy to burned.

Once cooked, remove the chips from the oven and let them cool on a wire rack to enable them to crisp up more.

Serve the baked sweet potato chips as a healthy snack choice.

These baked sweet potato chips are a tasty and guilt-free solution to fulfill your appetite for crispy nibbles. The inherent sweetness of sweet potatoes, mixed with savory spices, gives a pleasant taste profile. Enjoy these chips as a healthier alternative to typical potato chips while keeping your blood pressure objectives in mind.

This chapter presents a range of appetizer and snack dishes that concentrate on taste, texture, and nutrition. Whether it's the refreshing cucumber and yogurt dip, the spicy roasted red pepper hummus, or the satisfying baked sweet potato chips, these selections give alternatives to sodium-laden and harmful snacks. Incorporating these dishes into your diet may contribute to your general well-being and help maintain appropriate blood pressure levels.

CHAPTER 3
SOUPS AND SALADS

Minestrone Soup with Whole Grain Pasta

In this part, the cookbook gives a recipe for hearty and healthful Minestrone incorporating whole-grain pasta. Packed with veggies, lentils, and whole grains, this soup is a nourishing and savory alternative that promotes a blood pressure-friendly diet.

Ingredients:

1 tablespoon olive oil

1 medium onion, diced

2 cloves of garlic, minced 2 carrots, diced 2 celery stalks, diced 1 zucchini, diced 1 cup green beans, trimmed and sliced into bite-sized pieces

1 can (14 ounces) chopped tomatoes

4 cups vegetable or chicken broth (low-sodium if available)

1 teaspoon dried basil

1 teaspoon dried oregano

½ teaspoon dried thyme

½ cup whole grain pasta (such as whole wheat or brown rice spaghetti)

1 can (15 ounces) kidney beans, drained and rinsed

Salt and pepper to taste

Fresh basil or parsley, chopped (for garnish)

Instructions:

In a large saucepan, heat the olive oil over medium heat.

Add the chopped onion and minced garlic to the saucepan. Sauté for 2-3 minutes until the onion turns transparent and aromatic.

Add the chopped carrots, celery, zucchini, and green beans to the saucepan. Cook for another 5 minutes, stirring regularly, until the veggies begin to soften.

Stir in the chopped tomatoes, vegetable or chicken broth, dried basil, dry oregano, and dried thyme. Bring the mixture to a boil, then decrease the heat to low.

Simmer the soup uncovered for approximately 15 minutes to enable the flavors to melt together.

Add the whole-grain pasta and kidney beans to the pot. Cook for a further 10-12 minutes, or until the pasta is al dente.

Season the soup with salt and pepper to taste.

Ladle the Minestrone into dishes and decorate them with fresh basil or parsley.

Serve the soup warm and enjoy the soothing and healthful tastes.

This Minestrone dish shows the natural benefits of veggies, legumes, and nutritious grains. The inclusion of whole-grain pasta provides fiber and minerals while making the soup substantial and enjoyable. Enjoy this nutritious and tasty soup as a satisfying meal that supports your blood pressure objectives.

Quinoa and Vegetable Salad with Lemon Vinaigrette

A recipe for a vivid and refreshing quinoa and veggie salad with a zesty lemon vinaigrette. Packed with bright veggies and protein-rich quinoa, this salad delivers a nutrient-dense and tasty alternative for a blood pressure-friendly dinner.

Ingredients:

1 cup cooked quinoa

1 cup cherry tomatoes, halved

1 cucumber, diced

1 bell pepper, chopped (any color)

½ red onion, thinly sliced

¼ cup fresh parsley, chopped ¼ cup fresh mint leaves, chopped

Juice of 1 lemon

2 tablespoons extra virgin olive oil

1 clove of garlic, minced

Salt and pepper to taste

Instructions:

In a large mixing dish, add the cooked quinoa, cherry tomatoes, diced cucumber, diced bell pepper, sliced red onion, chopped parsley, and chopped mint leaves.

In a separate bowl, mix the lemon juice, extra virgin olive oil, minced garlic, salt, and pepper to create the lemon vinaigrette.

Pour the lemon vinaigrette over the quinoa and veggie combination.

Toss the salad carefully to ensure all the components are covered with the vinaigrette and properly incorporated.

Taste the salad and adjust the spices if required.

enable the salad to rest at room temperature for approximately 15 minutes to enable the flavors to melt together.

Serve the quinoa and veggie salad as a pleasant and healthy side dish or as a light main meal.

This quinoa and vegetable salad demonstrates the flexibility of quinoa as a nutrient-dense grain that mixes nicely with vivid veggies and tangy lemon vinaigrette. It's a tasty and savory meal that is low in salt and saturated fats, making it great for maintaining good blood pressure.

Watermelon and Feta Salad with Mint

 A recipe for a nice and sunny Watermelon and Feta Salad with a dash of mint. This salad mixes the natural sweetness of watermelon with the saltiness of feta cheese, providing a wonderful contrast of tastes while being low in sodium.

Ingredients:

4 cups cubed watermelon, cold

½ cup crumbled feta cheese

¼ cup fresh mint leaves, torn into tiny pieces

Juice of 1 lime

1 tablespoon extra-virgin olive oil

Freshly ground black pepper to taste

Instructions:

In a large serving dish, mix the cubed watermelon, crumbled feta cheese, and torn mint leaves.

In a small bowl, mix the lime juice and extra virgin olive oil to make a simple dressing.

Sprinkle the dressing over the watermelon, feta, and mint combination.

Gently toss the salad to coat all the ingredients with the dressing.

Season the salad with freshly chopped black pepper to taste.

Serve the Watermelon and Feta Salad chilled as a pleasant side dish or as a light and hydrating snack.

This Watermelon and Feta Salad is a great blend of sweet and salty tastes, with a touch of freshness from the mint. The watermelon gives moisture and important minerals, while the feta cheese adds a tart touch. Enjoy this salad as a pleasant complement to your meals while supporting your blood pressure objectives.

Chapter 3 presents a selection of soup and salad dishes that promote taste, nutrition, and diversity. Whether it's the soothing Minestrone, the brilliant Quinoa and Vegetable Salad, or the delightful Watermelon and Feta Salad, these dishes are meant to fuel your body while maintaining a blood pressure-friendly diet.

CHAPTER 4
MAIN COURSES

Grilled Chicken Breast with Herbed Quinoa

A tasty and lean main dinner with grilled chicken breast eaten with herbed quinoa. This recipe mixes lean protein with a healthy whole grain, offering a well-rounded and delicious meal.

Ingredients:

2 boneless, skinless chicken breasts

1 tablespoon olive oil

1 teaspoon dried Italian herbs (such as basil, oregano, and thyme)

Salt and pepper to taste

1 cup cooked quinoa

2 tablespoons fresh parsley, chopped

1 tablespoon fresh lemon juice

Lemon wedges (for serving)

Instructions:

Preheat a grill or grill pan over medium-high heat.

Rub the chicken breasts with olive oil, dried Italian herbs, salt, and pepper, ensuring they are equally covered.

Place the seasoned chicken breasts on the prepared grill or grill pan and cook for approximately 6-8 minutes on each side, or until the internal temperature reaches 165°F (75°C). Cooking times may vary based on the thickness of the chicken breasts.

Once done, take the chicken breasts from the grill and let them rest for a few minutes before slicing.

Meanwhile, in a mixing dish, add the cooked quinoa, chopped parsley, fresh lemon juice, salt, and pepper. Mix thoroughly to combine the flavors.

Serve the sliced grilled chicken breast over a bed of herbed quinoa.

Garnish with more fresh parsley and serve with lemon wedges for squeezing over the chicken, if preferred.

This grilled chicken breast with herbed quinoa delivers a lean dose of protein and whole-grain deliciousness. The herbed quinoa adds flavor and texture, making it a wonderful companion to the delicate and flavorful chicken. This main dish delivers a well-balanced meal while matching a blood pressure-friendly diet.

Baked Salmon with Dill Sauce

Baked fish with a tart and refreshing dill sauce. This recipe accentuates the advantages of fatty fish, like salmon, which is rich in omega-3 fatty acids, while offering a blast of flavor from the dill sauce.

Ingredients:

2 salmon fillets

1 tablespoon olive oil

Salt and pepper to taste

1 tablespoon fresh dill, chopped

2 tablespoons plain Greek yogurt

1 teaspoon Dijon mustard

Juice of ½ lemon

Instructions:

Preheat the oven to 375°F (190°C) and line a baking sheet with parchment paper.

Place the salmon fillets on the prepared baking sheet.

Drizzle the salmon with olive oil, then season with salt, pepper, and chopped fresh dill.

Bake the salmon in the preheated oven for approximately 12-15 minutes, or until it flakes easily with a fork and reaches an internal temperature of 145°F (63°C).

While the salmon is baking, create the dill sauce by mixing the Greek yogurt, Dijon mustard, lemon juice, and more chopped fresh dill in a small dish. Mix thoroughly to mix.

Once the salmon is done, take it from the oven and let it rest for a few minutes.

Serve the roasted salmon fillets with a dab of the dill sauce on top.

Garnish with more fresh dill, if preferred.

Enjoy the tasty and heart-healthy baked fish with the zesty dill sauce.

This baked salmon with dill sauce dish provides a lovely method to integrate omega-3 fatty acids into your diet while enjoying a tasty and healthy dinner. The acidic dill sauce enhances the rich taste of the salmon, producing a perfect equilibrium. This main course selection is well-suited for people looking to maintain appropriate blood pressure levels.

Lentil and Vegetable Curry

Hearty and delicious lentil and vegetable curry. This plant-based main course is filled with protein, fiber, and a variety of veggies, making it a fulfilling and healthy alternative for a blood pressure-friendly diet.

Ingredients:

1 tablespoon coconut oil or olive oil

1 big onion, chopped

3 cloves of garlic, minced

1 tablespoon fresh ginger, grated

2 tablespoons curry powder

1 teaspoon ground cumin

1 teaspoon ground turmeric

½ teaspoon ground coriander

¼ teaspoon cayenne pepper (optional, for heat)

1 cup dry green or brown lentils, washed

3 cups vegetable broth (low-sodium if available)

1 can (14 ounces) chopped tomatoes

2 cups mixed veggies (such as carrots, bell peppers, cauliflower, and peas)

Salt and pepper to taste

Fresh cilantro, chopped (for garnish)

Cooked brown rice or whole wheat naan (for serving)

Instructions:

In a big saucepan, heat the coconut oil or olive oil over medium heat.

Add the chopped onion, minced garlic, and grated ginger to the saucepan. Sauté for approximately 5 minutes until the onion turns translucent and the aromatics are fragrant.

Stir in the curry powder, powdered cumin, ground turmeric, ground coriander, and cayenne pepper (if using). Cook for an extra minute to roast the spices and unleash their flavors.

Add the rinsed lentils, vegetable broth, and diced tomatoes (with their juices) to the saucepan. Bring the mixture to a boil, then decrease the heat to low and cover the saucepan.

Simmer the lentil mixture for approximately 20 minutes, or until the lentils are soft but not mushy.

Stir in the mixed veggies and continue to simmer for a further 10-15 minutes until the vegetables are cooked to your preferred degree of softness.

Season the lentil and vegetable curry with salt and pepper to taste.

Serve the dish over cooked brown rice or with whole wheat naan.

Garnish with fresh chopped cilantro for extra taste and freshness.

This lentil and vegetable curry dish highlights the flexibility and nutritional advantages of legumes and vegetables. Packed with plant-based protein, fiber, and an assortment of spices, this curry delivers a full and savory main course while sticking to a blood pressure-friendly diet.

Main course dishes that highlight lean meats, nutritious grains, and an abundance of veggies. Whether it's the grilled chicken breast with herbed quinoa, the baked fish with dill sauce, or the lentil and vegetable curry, these recipes provide both taste and nutrition while supporting your attempts to maintain good blood pressure levels.

CHAPTER 5
SIDES AND VEGETABLES

Steamed Broccoli with Garlic and Lemon

The cookbook gives a simple but delectable recipe for cooked broccoli with garlic and lemon. This side dish showcases the natural taste of broccoli while adding a dash of garlic and tanginess from a fresh lemon.

Ingredients:

1 head of broccoli, sliced into florets

2 cloves of garlic, minced

1 tablespoon olive oil

Juice of ½ lemon

Salt and pepper to taste

Instructions:

Fill a big saucepan with approximately an inch of water and set a steamer basket inside.

Bring the water to a boil over medium heat.

Add the broccoli florets to the steamer basket and cover the pot. Steam for roughly 5-7 minutes, or until the broccoli is soft but still brilliant green. Avoid overcooking to retain nutrients.

While the broccoli is steaming, heat the olive oil in a small pan over medium heat.

Add the minced garlic to the pan and sauté for approximately 1-2 minutes until fragrant and faintly brown. Be cautious not to burn the garlic.

Once the broccoli is cooked, move it to a serving dish.

Drizzle the sautéed garlic and olive oil mixture over the steaming broccoli.

Squeeze fresh lemon juice over the broccoli and season with salt and pepper to taste.

Toss gently to coat the broccoli with the seasonings.

Serve the steamed broccoli with garlic and lemon as a healthful and appetizing side dish.

This steamed broccoli with garlic and lemon dish highlights the simplicity of preparation while keeping the natural aromas and minerals of the broccoli. The addition of garlic and lemon enriches the flavor and adds a pleasant twist. This side dish works nicely with a variety of main dishes, adding to a balanced and blood-pressure-friendly dinner.

Roasted Brussels Sprouts with Balsamic Glaze

Roasted Brussels sprouts with a wonderful balsamic glaze. This side dish turns Brussels sprouts into delicate, caramelized pieces with a dash of tanginess from the glaze.

Ingredients:

1 pound Brussels sprouts, trimmed and halved

2 tablespoons olive oil

Salt and pepper to taste

2 tablespoons balsamic vinegar

1 teaspoon honey or maple syrup (optional, for sweetness)

Instructions:

Preheat the oven to 400°F (200°C) and line a baking sheet with parchment paper.

In a large dish, mix the halved Brussels sprouts with olive oil, salt, and pepper until they are uniformly coated.

Arrange the Brussels sprouts in a single layer on the prepared baking sheet.

Roast the Brussels sprouts in the preheated oven for about 20-25 minutes, or until they are soft and caramelized. Flip them halfway through the cooking time for even browning.

While the Brussels sprouts are roasting, make the balsamic glaze. In a small saucepan, mix the balsamic vinegar and honey or maple syrup (if using).

Bring the mixture to a simmer over medium heat and cook for approximately 5 minutes, or until the glaze has decreased and thickened somewhat. Stir periodically to avoid burning.

Once the Brussels sprouts are roasted, take them from the oven and transfer them to a serving dish.

Drizzle the balsamic glaze over the roasted Brussels sprouts.

Toss carefully to ensure the sprouts are covered with the glaze.

Serve the roasted Brussels sprouts with balsamic glaze as a tasty and healthful side dish.

This roasted Brussels sprouts dish enhances the basic vegetable by roasting it to perfection and adding a sweet and tangy balsamic sauce. The roasting procedure amplifies the natural sweetness of Brussels sprouts while the glaze provides a wonderful blast of flavor. This side dish provides a delightful way to add veggies to your meals while keeping a blood pressure-friendly diet.

Garlic and Herb Roasted Sweet Potatoes

This side dish has the natural sweetness of sweet potatoes coupled with savory garlic and fragrant herbs, resulting in a pleasant and nutrient-rich complement to your dinner.

Ingredients:

2 big sweet potatoes, peeled and cut into cubes

2 tablespoons olive oil

2 cloves of garlic, minced

1 teaspoon dried rosemary

1 teaspoon dried thyme

Salt and pepper to taste

Instructions:

Preheat the oven to 425°F (220°C) and line a baking sheet with parchment paper.

In a large bowl, mix the sweet potato cubes with olive oil, chopped garlic, dried rosemary, dried thyme, salt, and pepper until they are thoroughly coated.

Spread the seasoned sweet potatoes in a single layer on the prepared baking sheet.

Roast the sweet potatoes in the preheated oven for about 25-30 minutes, or until they are soft and caramelized. Stir them midway through the cooking time for even browning.

Once roasted, remove the sweet potatoes from the oven and transfer them to a serving dish.

Serve the garlic and herb-roasted sweet potatoes as a delightful and healthful side dish.

This garlic and herb-roasted sweet potato dish mixes the natural sweetness of sweet potatoes with the savory tastes of garlic, rosemary, and thyme. The roasting procedure amplifies the taste and provides a caramelized surface while preserving a delicate and sensitive core. Enjoy these delectable roasted sweet potatoes as a healthful complement to your meals while supporting your blood pressure objectives.

CHAPTER 6
DESSERT
Mixed Berry Parfait with Greek Yogurt

Refreshing and guilt-free mixed berry parfait with Greek yogurt. This dish mixes the sweetness of mixed berries with the smoothness of Greek yogurt, delivering a wonderful treat while keeping your blood pressure objectives in mind.

Ingredients:

1 cup mixed berries (strawberries, blueberries, raspberries)

1 cup plain Greek yogurt

2 tablespoons honey or maple syrup

¼ cup granola (optional, for additional crunch)

Fresh mint leaves (for garnish)

Instructions:

In a bowl, mix the Greek yogurt and honey or maple syrup until fully blended.

Rinse the mixed berries and carefully wipe them dry with a paper towel.

Take serving cups or bowls and begin piling the ingredients. Start with a dollop of Greek yogurt mixture at the bottom of each glass.

Add a layer of mixed berries on top of the yogurt.

Repeat the layers of yogurt and berries until the glasses are full, culminating with a layer of mixed berries on top.

Sprinkle granola over the last berry layer for extra texture and crunch.

Garnish with fresh mint leaves.

Place the parfaits in the refrigerator to cool for at least 30 minutes before serving.

Serve the mixed berry parfait cold as a lovely and healthful dessert alternative.

This mixed fruit parfait with Greek yogurt is a delightful and healthy treat that mixes the natural sweetness of berries with the protein-rich creaminess of Greek yogurt. It's a guilt-free indulgence that enables you to indulge in a tasty dessert while keeping a blood pressure-friendly diet.

Dark Chocolate Avocado Mousse

For a thick and creamy dark chocolate avocado mousse. This dessert blends the benefits of avocados with the enjoyment of dark chocolate, resulting in a delectable treat that is surprisingly healthful.

Ingredients:

2 ripe avocados

¼ cup unsweetened cocoa powder

¼ cup pure maple syrup or honey

2 tablespoons almond milk (or your choice of milk)

1 teaspoon vanilla extract

Pinch of salt

Fresh berries (for garnish)

Instructions:

Cut the avocados in half and remove the pits. Scoop out the flesh and throw it in a blender or food processor.

Add the cocoa powder, maple syrup or honey, almond milk, vanilla extract, and salt to the blender or food processor.

Blend or process until the mixture is smooth and creamy, scraping down the sides as required.

Taste the mousse and adjust the sweetness if required by adding additional maple syrup or honey.

Transfer the dark chocolate avocado mousse to separate serving dishes or glasses.

Cover and refrigerate for at least 2 hours to enable the mousse to solidify and cold.

Before serving, garnish each plate with fresh berries.

Serve the dark chocolate avocado mousse cooled as a delightful and health-conscious dessert alternative.

This dark chocolate avocado mousse is a terrific way to fulfill your chocolate cravings while combining the health benefits of avocados. The creaminess of the avocado gives a velvety texture, while the dark chocolate adds depth and richness. Indulge in this guilt-free dessert that supports your blood pressure-friendly eating plan.

Baked Apples with Cinnamon and Walnuts

Baked apples with a wonderful blend of cinnamon and walnuts. This dish is warm, cozy, and full of natural sweetness, making it a pleasant treat that corresponds with your blood pressure objectives.

Ingredients:

2 apples (such as Granny Smith or Honeycrisp)

2 teaspoons chopped walnuts

1 tablespoon pure maple syrup or honey

1 teaspoon ground cinnamon

Pinch of nutmeg

Pinch of salt

Plain Greek yogurt or vanilla ice cream (optional, for serving)

Instructions:

Preheat the oven to 375°F (190°C) and prepare a baking dish with parchment paper.

Cut off the top of each apple and core the middle, forming a well for the filling.

In a small bowl, mix the chopped walnuts, maple syrup or honey, ground cinnamon, nutmeg, and salt until thoroughly blended.

Spoon the walnut mixture into the cavities of the apples, distributing it equally between them.

Place the packed apples in the prepared baking dish.

Bake in the preheated oven for about 30-35 minutes, or until the apples are soft and the filling is bubbling.

Remove the roasted apples from the oven and allow them cool for a few minutes before serving.

Serve the baked apples as they are or with a dollop of plain Greek yogurt or a scoop of vanilla ice cream for added pleasure.

These baked apples with cinnamon and walnuts create a comfortable and tasty dessert that honors the natural sweetness of apples while adding warm and cozy spices. The inclusion of walnuts adds a wonderful crunch and a dose of healthy fats. Enjoy this wonderful dessert as a healthier alternative that fulfills your sweet taste while matching a blood pressure-friendly diet.

Dessert dishes that offer healthier alternatives to conventional sweet delights. Whether it's the refreshing mixed berry parfait with Greek yogurt, the rich dark chocolate avocado mousse, or the cozy baked apples with cinnamon and walnuts, these desserts deliver a combination of tastes and nutrients while supporting your blood pressure objectives.

CHAPTER 7
BEVERAGES

Green Smoothie

A recipe for a delicious and nutrient-packed green smoothie. This beverage mixes leafy greens, fruits, and a hint of natural sweetness, delivering a wonderful way to integrate more greens into your diet.

Ingredients:

1 cup fresh spinach or kale leaves

1 ripe banana, peeled

1 cup frozen mango chunks

½ cup plain Greek yogurt

1 tbsp chia seeds

1 cup almond milk (or your choice of milk)

1 tablespoon honey or maple syrup (optional, for extra sweetness)

Instructions:

Place the fresh spinach or kale leaves in a blender.

Add the ripe banana, frozen mango pieces, plain Greek yogurt, chia seeds, almond milk, and honey or maple syrup (if using) to the blender.

Blend on high speed until all the ingredients are fully incorporated and the smoothie achieves a creamy smoothness.

If the smoothie is too thick, you may add extra almond milk to obtain your preferred consistency.

Taste the smoothie and adjust the sweetness by adding extra honey or maple syrup if required.

Pour the green smoothie into a glass and serve immediately.

Enjoy this refreshing and nutrient-packed beverage as a healthy start to your day or as a restorative snack.

This green smoothie is a wonderful method to improve your diet of leafy greens and fruits. Packed with vitamins, minerals, and fiber, this smoothie gives a refreshing and invigorating boost while supporting your blood pressure-friendly eating plan.

Hibiscus Iced Tea

In this part, the cookbook includes a recipe for a vivid and tasty hibiscus iced tea. Known for its possible blood pressure-lowering effects, hibiscus tea is a delightful and health-conscious beverage option.

Ingredients:

4 cups water

¼ cup dried hibiscus blossoms

2 tablespoons honey or maple syrup (optional, for sweetness)

Juice of 1 lime or lemon (optional, for extra tanginess)

Ice cubes

Fresh mint leaves or lime wedges (for garnish)

Instructions:

In a saucepan, bring the water to a boil.

Add the dried hibiscus blossoms to the boiling water and decrease the heat to low.

Let the hibiscus blossoms soak in the water for around 10-15 minutes.

Remove the skillet from heat and filter the hibiscus tea into a pitcher, discarding the flowers.

Stir in honey or maple syrup (if using) until it melts completely.

Allow the hibiscus tea to cool to room temperature, then refrigerate until cooled.

Once cold, pour the hibiscus tea into glasses packed with ice cubes.

Squeeze in fresh lime or lemon juice (if preferred) for extra tanginess.

Garnish each glass with fresh mint leaves or lime wedges.

Stir thoroughly before enjoying this delightful and health-conscious hibiscus iced tea.

This hibiscus iced tea is a delicious and vivid beverage alternative that not only quenches your thirst but also gives possible advantages for maintaining good blood pressure levels. The natural tanginess of hibiscus mixed with a hint of sweetness provides a tasty and refreshing drink.

Infused Water with Citrus and Mint

In this part, the cookbook gives a recipe for infused water with citrus and mint. This hydrating and delicious beverage adds a burst of flavor to ordinary water, making it a fantastic alternative for keeping hydrated while enjoying a taste of citrus and mint.

Ingredients:

4 cups water

1 lemon, thinly sliced

1 lime, finely sliced

Handful of fresh mint leaves

Ice cubes

Instructions:

In a pitcher, add the water, lemon slices, lime slices, and fresh mint leaves.

Stir carefully to unleash the flavors of the citrus and mint.

Refrigerate the infused water for at least 1 hour to enable the flavors to melt together.

When ready to serve, fill glasses with ice cubes.

Pour the infused water into the glasses, making sure to include a few citrus slices and mint leaves in each glass.

Stir well and enjoy this pleasant and hydrating-infused water.

This infused water with citrus and mint adds a burst of flavor to ordinary water, making it an attractive and hydrating beverage alternative. The citrus slices infuse the water with delightful flavors, while the mint leaves add a cold and energizing twist. Sip on this infused water throughout the day to remain hydrated while enjoying a bit of natural flavor.

A range of beverage recipes complements a blood pressure-friendly diet. Whether it's the nutrient-packed green smoothie, the refreshing hibiscus iced tea, or the infused water with citrus and mint, these beverages give delectable alternatives to sugary and high-sodium drinks. Enjoy these refreshing and hydrating drinks as part of a balanced and health-conscious lifestyle.

CHAPTER 8
SNACKS & SMALL BITES

Roasted Chickpeas with Spices

In this part, the cookbook gives a recipe for roasted chickpeas with a fragrant combination of spices. This snack alternative is filled with fiber and plant-based protein, making it a tasty and nutritious choice for controlling hunger between meals.

Ingredients:

1 can (15 ounces) chickpeas (garbanzo beans), drained and rinsed

1 tablespoon olive oil

1 teaspoon ground cumin

1 teaspoon paprika

½ teaspoon garlic powder

½ teaspoon chili powder (optional, for heat)

Salt to taste

Instructions:

Preheat the oven to 400°F (200°C) and line a baking sheet with parchment paper.

Rinse and drain the chickpeas, then pat them dry with a paper towel.

In a mixing bowl, combine the dry chickpeas, olive oil, ground cumin, paprika, garlic powder, chili sauce (if using), and salt.

Toss the chickpeas in the spice mixture until they are uniformly covered.

Spread the seasoned chickpeas in a single layer on the prepared baking sheet.

Roast the chickpeas in the preheated oven for about 25-30 minutes, or until they are crispy and golden brown.

Remove the chickpeas from the oven and allow them cool for a few minutes before consuming.

Serve the roasted chickpeas as a tasty and protein-rich snack.

These roasted chickpeas with spices provide a crispy and tasty snack choice that is high in fiber and plant-based protein. The combination of spices provides a savory and fragrant flavor, making them a pleasurable and blood-pressure-friendly alternative to processed munchies.

Veggie Sticks with Hummus

A recipe for vegetable sticks with a creamy and tasty hummus dip. This snack alternative is low in calories and rich in nutrients, giving a nutritious and crunchy approach to fulfill your desires.

Ingredients:

Assorted fresh veggies (carrots, cucumbers, bell peppers, celery, etc.)

1 cup canned chickpeas (garbanzo beans), drained and rinsed

2 tablespoons tahini (sesame paste)

2 teaspoons lemon juice

1 clove garlic, minced

2 tablespoons extra virgin olive oil

Salt and pepper to taste

Fresh parsley or paprika (for garnish)

Instructions:

Wash and chop the raw veggies into sticks or bite-sized pieces.

In a food processor or blender, mix the drained and rinsed chickpeas, tahini, lemon juice, chopped garlic, extra virgin olive oil, salt, and pepper.

Process the ingredients until smooth and creamy, adding a little water if required to obtain the desired consistency.

Taste the hummus and adjust the spice if required.

Transfer the hummus to a serving dish and top with fresh parsley or a sprinkle of paprika.

Arrange the veggie sticks around the hummus dish or serve them on a separate tray.

Serve the vegetable sticks with hummus as a wholesome and tasty snack.

This vegetable sticks with hummus dish provides a colorful and healthful snack choice that is high in vitamins, minerals, and fiber. The crisp texture of fresh veggies mixed with the creamy and protein-rich hummus offers a pleasant and blood-pressure-friendly snack.

Greek Yogurt with Berries and Nuts

Greek yogurt with a mix of berries and almonds. This snack choice is filled with protein, antioxidants, and healthy fats, giving a nutritious and tasty approach to keep your energy levels up.

Ingredients:

1 cup plain Greek yogurt

½ cup mixed berries (strawberries, blueberries, raspberries)

2 tablespoons mixed nuts (almonds, walnuts, cashews, etc.), chopped

1 tablespoon honey or maple syrup (optional, for extra sweetness)

Instructions:

In a serving dish or glass, scoop the plain Greek yogurt.

Top the yogurt with mixed berries and chopped almonds.

Drizzle honey or maple syrup over the yogurt and toppings for extra sweetness, if preferred.

Stir carefully to incorporate the ingredients or eat them stacked.

Serve the Greek yogurt with berries and almonds as a pleasant and protein-rich snack.

CHAPTER 9
MEAL PLANNING AND TIPS

Benefits of Meal Planning for Blood Pressure Management

In this part, the recipe book highlights the necessity of meal planning for good blood pressure control. Planning your meals may help you make better food choices, guarantee a balanced diet, and maintain constant salt and nutrient consumption.

Meal planning enables you to:

Control salt Intake: By preparing your meals, you may be careful of the salt concentration in the items you use. High salt consumption is commonly connected to high blood pressure, so preparing meals that incorporate fresh foods and low-sodium options will help you control your blood pressure more successfully.

Incorporate Nutrient-Rich Foods: A well-planned meal may contain a range of nutrient-rich foods such as fruits, vegetables, whole grains, lean meats, and healthy fats. These foods include critical vitamins, minerals, antioxidants, and fiber, which play a key role in supporting overall cardiovascular health.

Achieve Balanced Meals: Meal planning helps you generate well-balanced meals that have the proper amount of carbs, proteins, and fats. This balance supports consistent blood sugar levels and helps you feel satiated, lessening the desire to grab harmful foods.

Avoid Unhealthy Foods: When you prepare your meals, you have greater control over the foods you use. You may avoid processed meals heavy in harmful fats, added sugars, and artificial additives. Instead, you may pick full, unprocessed meals that feed your body and support your blood pressure objectives.

Save Time and Money: Planning meals may save you time and money. By developing a shopping list based on your meal plan, you may prevent impulsive purchases and decrease food waste.

Additionally, having pre-planned meals saves you the burden of picking what to prepare each day.

Tips for Blood Pressure-Friendly Meal Planning

In this part, the cookbook presents practical recommendations to assist you manage blood pressure-friendly meal planning:

Create a Weekly Meal Plan: Dedicate some time each week to plan your meals for the next week. Consider your schedule, available ingredients, and nutritional choices. Aim for a balance of diverse food categories and tastes.

Variety of Fruits and Vegetables: Aim to incorporate a broad assortment of fruits and veggies into your meal plan. They are rich in important nutrients, fiber, and antioxidants that improve heart health. Incorporate them into salads, soups, smoothies, and side dishes.

Opt for Lean Proteins: Choose lean protein sources such as skinless chicken, fish, lentils, and tofu. These selections are lower in saturated fat and include key nutrients like omega-3 fatty acids. Be aware of portion quantities to maintain a balanced diet.

Emphasize Whole Grains: Replace refined grains with whole grains such as brown rice, quinoa, whole wheat pasta, and whole grain bread. Whole grains offer more fiber and minerals, which may help decrease blood pressure and enhance overall cardiovascular health.

Limit Sodium Intake: Read food labels carefully and seek low-sodium options when available. Season your dishes using herbs, spices, and other tasty items instead of depending on salt. Cooking from scratch helps you to regulate the salt amount in your meals.

Cook in Bulk and Freeze Portions: Consider batch preparing and freezing individual portions of meals for busy days. This helps you have healthy, home-cooked choices easily accessible, avoiding dependency on harmful takeout or processed meals.

Stay Hydrated: Remember to drink enough water throughout the day. Hydration is vital for maintaining normal blood pressure levels. Consider infusing water with citrus pieces, cucumber, or herbs for extra taste and delight.

Practice Mindful Eating: When sitting down for meals, take your time to appreciate each mouthful and heed your body's hunger and fullness signals. Eating thoughtfully helps reduce overeating and improves healthier digestion.

Long-Term Lifestyle Changes

In this part, the cookbook highlights the necessity of long-term lifestyle changes in regulating blood pressure:

Regular Physical Activity: Alongside a good diet, frequent physical exercise plays a significant part in maintaining blood pressure. Engage in activities you love, such as vigorous walking, swimming, cycling, or yoga. Aim for at least 150 minutes of moderate-intensity exercise every week.

Stress Management: Chronic stress might lead to high blood pressure. Explore stress-reducing activities such as meditation, deep breathing techniques, writing, or indulging in hobbies. Find what works best for you to encourage relaxation and mental well-being.

Portion Control: Pay attention to portion sizes and practice mindful eating. Use smaller dishes and bowls to prevent overeating. Focus on eating until you feel content rather than too stuffed.

Seek Professional Guidance: If you have unique dietary requirements or health concerns, visit a trained dietician or healthcare practitioner. They may give tailored advice and help in regulating your blood pressure via dietary adjustments.

CONCLUSION

In conclusion, a cookbook developed to decrease high blood pressure is a great resource for anyone looking to take charge of their cardiovascular health. By making intentional decisions and including blood pressure-friendly dishes in daily meal planning, it is feasible to build a balanced and healthy diet that promotes normal blood pressure levels.

The recipes contained in such a cookbook stress complete, unprocessed foods, and highlight tasty combinations of fruits, vegetables, lean meats, whole grains, and heart-healthy fats. These components contain critical nutrients, fiber, antioxidants, and minerals that help with general cardiovascular well-being.

By limiting salt consumption, selecting potassium-rich foods, and adopting a diet low in saturated and trans fats, people may address critical dietary variables that affect blood pressure management. The cookbook encourages readers to produce tasty meals that value fresh foods, herbs, spices, and natural sweeteners, without losing flavor or pleasure.

Moreover, the cookbook highlights the need for meal planning, portion management, and mindful eating as vital components of a blood pressure-friendly lifestyle. It urges readers to create long-term lifestyle changes by including regular physical exercise, stress management strategies, and seeking expert help when required.

Ultimately, a cookbook for decreasing high blood pressure allows people to make educated food choices that favorably benefit their cardiovascular health. By embracing the recipes, meal planning suggestions, and lifestyle recommendations inside the cookbook's pages, readers may begin on a path towards better blood pressure control, greater well-being, and a healthier future.

Printed in Great Britain
by Amazon